OMNIBUS PRESS PRESENTS

the unofficial story of

FALL OUT BOY

JESSE SABA

OMNIBUS PRESS

OMNIBUS PRESS

Part of **The Music Sales Group**
New York/London/Paris/Sydney/Copenhagen/Berlin/Tokyo/Madrid

Copyright © 2007 Omnibus Press

ISBN 978-0-8256-7337-5
Order No. OP51942

Exclusive Distributors:
Music Sales Corporation
257 Park Avenue South, New York, NY 10010 USA

Music Sales Limited
14-15 Berners St., London W1T 3LJ United Kingdom

Music Sales Pty. Limited
120 Rothschild Street, Rosebery, Sydney, NSW 2018 Australia

Picture research, cover and book design by Sarah Nesenjuk

Photo Credits: All photographers represented by WireImage.com except where otherwise noted.

Front Cover: Stephen Lovekin
Back Cover: Ron Wolfson

Skip Bolen: 86. Larry Busacca: 1. Robb D. Cohen / Retna, LTD: 46, 48. Jemal Countess: 61. Rick Diamond: 49.
Ron Galella:70. Gary Gershoff: 56, 78. Stephen Lovekin: 39. Dan MacMedan: 65. Jeffrey Mayer: 12, 30. Kevin
Mazur: 62, 88, 67. Soren McCarty: 53. Al Messerschmidt: 23, 82. Frank Mullen: 4. Paul Natkin: 29. Sam Newman:
3, 84. Bennett Raglin: 80. Chuck Rydlewski: 50. John Sciulli: 16, 18, 74, 83. James Sharrock: 26. John Shearer: 20,
32, 68. Sean Smith: 6. Andy Stubbs: 10, 45, 52. John Parra: 9. Theo Wargo: 66, 72. Paul Warner: 54, 77. Mychal
Watts: 15, 42, 59. Kirsty Pargeter/istock.com: background paper. Dave Smith/istock.com: title scroll

Printed in the United States of America
Visit Omnibus Press at www.omnibuspress.com

TABLE OF CONTENTS

INTRODUCTION

To hear super cute bass player Pete Wentz tell it, Fall Out Boy would still be out there playing the clubs and making music… even if none of us cared enough to listen. And that's probably exactly why we can't get enough of these goofy guys next door who play "softcore" pop-punk with a bit of emo thrown in for good measure. There's no pretense; this quartet – singer Patrick Stump, bassist Pete Wentz, guitarist Joe Trohman and drummer Andrew Hurley – hail from the good side of the tracks in Chicago. They're pretty simple dudes. They love music and they dig communicating with their fans even more. It's the type of authenticity that earns loyal fans… the type who download every single the minute it's released, own every record and arrive hours early for the band's gig at the local arena.

Fall Out Boy appears to have it all, and yet, they're just like you and me with doubts and insecurities tied to just about everything. As Pete told *Rolling Stone*, "I feel confidence in myself, but at the same time there's these cracks in the façade and those little things underneath that are unstable." You'd think the climb to the top would have been easy for these kids that came from a fairly privileged background. But, you'd think wrong. It took an amazing amount of tenacity for this band to keep things together and play to anyone who would listen. They'd be on the road in their van for months at a time, sleeping on floors and living off of PB&J sandwiches. And just when fame and fortune came a knocking in 2005, the pressure overwhelmed Pete who attempted to kill himself with an Ativan overdose.

The future of the band swung in the balance but fans saved the day by embracing their album, *From Under the Cork Tree*. From there, Fall Out Boy was a stick of dynamite waiting to explode… and that they did in 2005 with a sell-out arena tour and a Grammy nomination for Best New Artist of the Year.

Fast forward to February 6, 2007. The band's latest effort, *Infinity on High*, is released in the U.S. amid a frenzy of activity in music stores everywhere and it

OVERCAST KIDS
OFFICIAL
FAN CLUB

Fall Out Boy hosts a special community for its most rabid followers with its Overcast Kids official fan club. For about $30 a year (as of winter 2007), you get access to Overcast's exclusive website that's packed with rare photos and videos, a members-only message board and store that sells FOB merch that you won't find elsewhere. You'll be the first to receive Fall Out Boy news, participate in contests and lay your hands on concert tickets before the general public. And, when you first join, you'll receive a gift box filled with goodies, including a T-shirt, sticker, pin, postcard, temporary tattoo and official membership card. Join now at *OvercastKids.com*.

seems the world is at their feet. But how did these four unassuming guys from the Midwest get here in the first place? Read on to learn the inside story of Fall Out Boy!

L-R: Joe Trohman, Patrick Stump, Pete Wentz and Andy Hurley.

CHAPTER ONE

IN THE
BEGINNING

U nlike other emo/pop-punk bands, the guys in Fall Out Boy did not have a
rough childhood. In fact, they pretty much lucked out… each having
been born to pretty cool parents in fairly affluent families.

The story of Fall Out Boy doesn't start with lead singer Patrick Stump or
charismatic bassist Pete Wentz for that matter. FOB's lineage actually began
when guitarist Joe Trohman suggested to Pete that the two form a band in their
hometown of Wilmette, IL. But, let's go back in time just a bit first.

Joseph Mark Trohman was born on September 1, 1984 in Hollywood, FL, but
he grew up on the east end of Cleveland, OH. He loved music right from the
start and played both trumpet and guitar. At the age of 12, Joe's family moved to
a Chicago suburb and he enrolled at Washburne Middle School. This is where he
joined a band before moving on to New Trier Township High School. He was in
the AV club (not as lame as it sounds) and played bass for a short time in a band
called Arma Angelus (coincidently with Pete Wentz, who would later also join
Joe in Fall Out Boy). Joe grew up as part of a well-to-do Jewish family – his
father is a cardiologist – and he was able to follow his interest in music by
listening to tons of records and joining bands himself.

With some band experience under his belt, Joe felt it was time to get serious and form a group to play the kind of music he loved: hardcore. In late 2000/early 2001, he approached his high school friend Pete Wentz who readily agreed to give it a go. A few days later, Joe was sipping a coffee at the café in Borders when he met part-time bookstore clerk Patrick Stump.

"I met Patrick [when I was having] a conversation about [tribal noise metal band] Neurosis in a Borders bookstore," Joe told MTV. "I was taking really loud 'cause I talk really loud about Neurosis and other metal stuff, and he happened to hear and came over and started talking to us. I ended up talking to him for an hour straight."

Joe and Patrick shared a love for the same music and Joe encouraged him to join his band as a drummer. As soon as Patrick auditioned however, it was clear that he'd make a much better lead singer and he abandoned his career as a drummer right then and there. At this point, the trio had no idea what the future would bring. They just wanted to play music, have some fun and maybe meet a pretty girl or two.

You'd think that Patrick Stump would've become the de facto leader of the band since he's the lead singer and songwriter. The only problem is that he feels so uncomfortable being the center of attention that he lets bassist Pete Wentz take care of any official "frontman" tasks, such as the bulk of interviews with the press or photo shoots. "I'm horribly uncomfortable with being the frontman," Patrick told *Rolling Stone*, "With Pete, I get to be the anti-frontman. There's not attention on me; I just get to sing. Pete loves photo shoots and I hate them. Of all the things I have to be self-conscious about, my looks are top of the heap." Even so, Patrick quickly became the cornerstone of the band as their lead singer, songwriter and backup guitarist.

While the world was rocking out to David Bowie's *Let's Dance*, Patrick was born in Glenview, IL on April 27, 1984. His parents named him Patrick Martin Stumph; he later dropped the "h" in his last name. Luckily, his family was into music and that surely had an affect on baby Patrick. His father, once a wannabe folk singer, ultimately took on a corporate job to meet the demands and responsibilities of being a family man.

During school, Patrick took part in any activity that was related to music and even played drums in a variety of bands, including Public Display of Infection, Xgrinding processZ and Patterson. He also wrote for the school magazine, *Channel Zero*, about social issues. (Patrick's belief in equality and diversity can still be seen today in Fall Out Boy's work.)

While Patrick isn't the youngest Fall Out Boy – guitarist Joe Trohman holds that distinction – Patrick was just a junior in high school when he was invited to join the band. That was the beginning of everything; and while he's never gone to college, he hasn't looked back either.

Pete Wentz is the oldest member of Fall Out Boy, having been born Peter Lewis Kingston Wentz III in Wilmette, IL on June 5, 1979. He lived in a killer neighborhood and his parents held down professional jobs: Dad was working as a lawyer while Mom was dean of admissions at a fancy private school. Things were good and Pete grew up pretty much like the rest of us in Middle America. He went to North Shore Country Day School and New Trier Township High School where he literally lived to play soccer. In fact, he was so good he made all-state!

He graduated high school in 1997 and went on to DePaul University right there in Chicago where his social conscience led him to become a political science major. During his high school and college years, he was in a slew of bands, including xfirstbornx, Arma Angelus, 7 Angels of the Apocalypse, Culture of Violence, xBirthrightx, Extinction, Forever Ended Today, Yellow Road Priest and Project Rocket. Pete told *Rolling Stone* that, "My childhood was pretty mundane. There was no tragic event, nobody got divorced, nobody died. I was bored a lot. I just skateboarded and was into fireworks and music."

When he got together with Joe Trohman to form a band, he didn't think anything of it, really. Sure, he'd be the bassist, main lyricist and backup singer, but he just really wanted to be in a band with his friends and have fun. "We started just goofing around," Pete told Jim DeRogatis of the *Chicago Sun-*

Times. "It was pretty much just a joke. We only started taking it more seriously as our friends started getting into it and saying, 'You guys are pretty good!'"

Pete had no idea that the success of the band would pull him away from college. He dropped out one semester before he was eligible to graduate.

So, what kind of music does Fall Out Boy actually play? That is a much-debated question to the chagrin of the band. They grew up as part of Chicago's hardcore scene, but others thought they had more of a pop-punk edge, like Green Day or Jimmy Eat World. The band itself has dubbed their genre "softcore," but they'd really prefer no label at all, as Pete explained to *University Wire*: "Honestly, to me we're like a hardcore band, or a softcore band. I kind of put us in a category of our own or with a few other bands. At the end of the day a label is a label, so whatever somebody wants to call us is fine. I don't think you should love or hate our music because you think we're pop-punk, or you think we're emo or you think we're whatever. Love or hate it because you like it or don't like it." Pete says that, ultimately, "We're in love with hooks, but at the same time, we like smart music. We've always considered ourselves 'softcore.'"

The more important question to ask, however, is why hardcore was embraced by a bunch of suburban kids in the first place. "The suburbs are so close to the danger and vibrancy of the city, but they don't have [either]," Patrick told the *Alternative Press* in 2005. "So you can see it go by, but you can't really experience it. It is one of those things, culturally, where the only thing you can rebel against is how confining the suburb is and how confining it is to live there." Teens across American can probably relate to that.

The trio didn't add a full-time drummer to their band until after their 2003 album *Evening Out with Your Girlfriend* was released. That's when Andy Hurley joined the team. Andy is a Milwaukee boy, born on May 31, 1980, and while he says he was a handful as a kid – and a pretty heavy drinker – he brought his current straightedge lifestyle to Fall Out Boy. In fact, Andy, Patrick and Pete all share this dedication and don't drink or do illegal drugs. Joe is the only band member that doesn't adhere to this strict policy. Pete explained a bit about his appreciation for going straightedge to the *Philadelphia Inquirer*, "A lot of my friends were into punk rock and drinking. At some point, I realized America is frat-boy culture. There's even one in the White House. It isn't punk rock if you're buying into that idea. You're just dressing differently." Sounds about right.

Andy is a rock solid drummer and was previously in the politically charged band, Racetraitor. (Pete was a member of that band as well for a while.) He loves life out on the road, but being a vegan can make it a bit challenging. Like everyone else in Fall Out Boy, he loves music, comic books and video games. A typical midwestern guy!

Together this quartet would pogo their way onto the charts and into the lives of millions of fans. And it all started with a three-song self-released demo in 2001.

chapter two

FOB DEMO
PRIMES THE PUMP

In 2001 – with the core band in place – Patrick, Pete and Joe hunkered down to practice and write some songs. They even released a DIY three-song demo with a scene from the 1984 movie, *The Karate Kid*, as cover art. Of course, now they all say they're embarrassed to hear those early attempts at making music! But the songs started buzzing around the Internet and Chicago-area fans, and others, took notice.

The band also began playing out… first at house parties and then at clubs in the area. In fact, the Chicago suburbs had become a hotbed for the punk/emo and hardcore movements, much like the New Jersey scene that inspired My Chemical Romance.

Fall Out Boy didn't even have its name when they first started gigging! But, a fan came to the rescue at a concert and named the band for the guys. Pete explained to MTV, "We were playing and we asked the crowd what they thought we should call ourselves. So a kid yelled out, 'Fall Out Boy,' and it stuck." The name is also a reference to the cartoon, *The Simpsons*. In the show, Bart Simpson's favorite superhero is Radioactive Man and his faithful sidekick is none other than Fallout Boy.

It's a pretty clever name that works on several levels and the guys can't imagine *not* being called Fall Out Boy. With this memorable moniker, the band kept plugging away and played in front of any audience that would have them. They started honing their performance skills, as well as their songwriting chops.

Around this time, the band made sure record labels had a copy of their

demo… not that any of the A&R execs actually ever *listened* to it. But the band would have the last laugh when a year or so later, these same A&R dudes were calling non-stop asking for Fall Out Boy's demo tape as Pete related to Jim DeRogatis of the *Chicago Sun-Times*: "We thought nobody would ever have a reaction, so we just started playing everywhere we could and giving our demo to everyone we could ever give it to. Eventually, we started to get a buzz and these labels started calling us back. All these labels that we had sent the demo to started calling us, and they'd be like, 'Send us a tape,' and I'd be like, 'You have it just sitting in your office and you've never listened to it!'"

The band thought the attention from the labels was pretty funny and cool, but they were more concerned with their fans at this point. To get to the next level, Fall Out Boy needed to release more music, and soon.

CHAPTER THREE

2002 BRINGS SPLIT

The spring of 2002 found Fall Out Boy busy working on new songs for the *Split* album. Created in conjunction with local band Project Rocket, the bands combined their resources for a record that would include three tunes from each outfit. Fall Out Boy selected "Growing Up," "Switchblades and Infidelity" and "Moving Pictures." Project Rocket recorded "Formula for Love," "You Charlatan" and "Someday." Jared Logan produced both bands and the album was released by indie label Uprising Records. When the record was first released, Project Rocket's songs were first on the track listing. When the album was reissued later, FOB got top billing.

The year went by in a blur as the band hustled to get gigs, mainly at Knights of Columbus halls in the North Shore suburbs of Chicago, and built a fan base. They played out wherever they could and for whoever would listen. Sometimes that meant to a crowd that numbered less than a dozen. But, the band persevered. They'd work the phones to book a gig and then pile in their less-than-reliable van to travel to the show. The van let them down on several occasions, according to Pete. "It was a tiny V6 that was running on three cylinders, and it was not getting enough air, so it would drive really slowly. We had to turn on the hot air to reach the speed limit, so we had the heat on all the time in 120-degree weather. It was so hot it melted the plastic molding around the windows. When it rained, we'd get all wet," he told MTV in November of 2003.

They played hundreds of shows in 2002 and started to gel as a live band. Each member showed incredible energy on stage: Andy was often just a blur behind his drum kit as Joe twirled across the stage – guitar in hand – while Pete perfected his stage banter. Patrick sang his lungs out each and every night and soon kids were telling all their friends – in person and online – about the righteous new band they heard the night before. The buzz was building.

chapter four

TAKE THIS
TO YOUR GRAVE

When 2003 hit, bassist Pete Wentz's biggest concern was finding a way to book gigs beyond the level of local club Fireside Bowl and into the likes of upscale Metro. He had no idea that the next 12 months would be pivotal to getting the band noticed not just in Chicago but across the nation. With fans happily enjoying Fall Out Boy's three songs on the *Split* LP, the band had worked hard over the past few months to write new material for their first full-length record on Uprising. The project reunited them with producer Jared Logan who whisked them away to Milwaukee to record from February to September 2002. The album titled *Evening Out with Your Girlfriend* was released on February 25, 2003. Fans knew it was something special right away. The songs included:

"Honorable Mention"
"Calm Before the Storm"
"Switchblades and Infidelity"
"Pretty in Punk"

"Growing Up"
"World's Not Waiting (For Five Tired Boys in a Broken Van)"
"Short, Fast and Loud"
"Moving Pictures"
"Parker Lewis Can't Lose (But I'm Gonna Give It My Best Shot)"

Right off the bat, fans will notice that these are perhaps some of the shortest titles for any Fall Out Boy songs! After all, "Our Lawyer Made Us Change the Name of This Song So We Wouldn't Get Sued" is a taste of the long-winded titles FOB currently uses!

When *Evening Out* premiered, national media did a double-take and started giving props to the Chicagoland quartet. Fuse and mtvU both embraced the album and played it all the time. While still not a household name, Fall Out Boy was making inroads across the nation and indie label Fueled by Ramen – based in Gainesville, FL – decided that FOB was just what the doctor ordered. Less Than Jake drummer Vinnie Balzano and John Janick – co-owners of the label – signed Fall Out Boy in a heartbeat after listening to *Evening Out*. In an interview with New Jersey's *Bergen Record*, Janick said, "I thought the band was awesome. There are very few bands that just from hearing a song you feel something special, like you've got to sign them right away, and they were one of those bands."

Lots of labels were actually talking with the band, but they liked what they heard from the guys at Fueled by Ramen. "You have to work twice as hard when you're in the Midwest," Pete confided to the *Arlington Daily Herald* in 2005, "In L.A., there are A&R guys who go to shows, but in the middle of the country, you have to be doing something really well. We were hungry." That's an understatement. Fall Out Boy played hard on the road, kept up with its fans online and made sure all the independent labels had heard their demo.

As mentioned, Fueled by Ramen wasn't the only record label that took notice of Fall Out Boy. Major label Island Records was so enamored with the boys that they put up a fair amount of money so the band could record, market and promote their forthcoming record on the Fueled imprint. The catch? Island would have first right of refusal on the band's next album. That seemed fair to the band and to executives at Fueled by Ramen and that's when things started to happen at light speed.

Drummer Andy Hurley joined Fall Out Boy right after the release of *Evening*

Out and was with the band when they played an all-important date in Austin at the industry's hottest music showcase, South by Southwest. At this point, the band had been touring nonstop and were starting to gain fans and friends in the industry, including *Chicago Sun-Times* music critic Jim DeRogatis. In a May 2003 interview, Pete told DeRogatis, "I have not slept in my bed for more than three days straight since January 1!" Not surprising, since Fall Out Boy always knew it would take a massive effort to reach out and become an integral part of the emo/punk movement. "We want to go out and earn the fans," Pete went on. "Often that's meant us playing to, like, two people and sleeping on the floor of our van at night, but I want to do it the right way. I don't want to be some created band. I think music is taking a turn toward real music again – like it did maybe with grunge – and I want to be a part of that movement. I don't want to be one of these pre-made bands."

So, with funds from both Fueled by Ramen and Island Records, Fall Out Boy set out to make its first "real" record at producer Butch Vig's Smart Studios in Madison, WI. They also worked at Rosebud Studios in Skokie, IL and mixed the tracks in Chicago at Gravity Studios. The band tapped Sean O'Keefe, of Lucky Boys Confusion and Motion City Soundtrack fame, to produce and mix the record, and Dominick Maita mastered it at New York City's Sterling Sound.

The band recorded what would turn out to be *Take This to Your Grave*. The songs on this album were at once honest and electrifying. The track list included:

"Tell That Mick He Just Made My List of Things to Do Today"
"Dead on Arrival"
"Grand Theft Autumn/Where Is Your Boy?"
"Saturday"
"Homesick at Space Camp"
"Sending Postcards from a Plane Crash (Wish You Were Here)"
"Chicago Is So Two Years Ago"
"The Pros and Cons of Breathing"
"Grenade Jumper"
"Calm Before the Storm"
"Reinventing the Wheel to Run Myself Over"
"The Patron Saint of Liars and Fakes"

Patrick, Joe, Andy and Pete were a bit overwhelmed working at a recording facility like Smart Studios that had such an illustrious past. "We went up there and the first second we walked in we saw the Platinum record on the wall for *Nevermind* [Nirvana] and we were like, 'What are we doing here?' But it was interesting," Pete told the *Chicago Sun-Times*, "because this was the first time where we actually had the chance to take our time. We had a budget to make errors, to chop parts and to go back and change things when we didn't like it. We had a vision for the record – we really went over it with a fine-tooth comb – and I hope that people can hear that when they listen to it."

Patrick says the album was a culmination of many years' work. He told MTV, "We did the three songs from the demo a year before we finished the record and kept working on the rest of the songs after that."

Standout tunes on this hook-filled treat include "Grand Theft Autumn/Where Is Your Boy?" and "Saturday." Both are still crowd favorites at FOB concerts.

What was the inspiration for the lyrics for these songs? Unfortunately for Pete, a horrible experience with a girlfriend triggered a lot of the gut-wrenching lines. See, he found out that his girlfriend cheated on him… with not one, but *two* of his best friends… on the same weekend. Ouch! The songs on *Take This to Your Grave* capture Pete's heartbreak, anger and confusion over the ordeal.

Besides the CD release on May 6, 2003, the band issued a limited edition vinyl 12-inch. In addition to the album tracks, it also contained a remix of "Grand Theft Autumn/Where Is Your Boy?" One thousand copies were pressed, 500 in camouflage green vinyl and the balance in black.

The songs on *Take This to Your Grave* were hot and everyone involved hoped the fans would react. They did. The record ultimately sold over 200,000 copies, an impressive feat for any independent band. The record also won the coveted Number One spot on *Alternative Press'* AP Reader Chart for several months during 2003.

Three singles were released: "Saturday," "Dead on Arrival" and "Grand Theft Autumn/Where Is Your Boy?" The band filmed videos for all three singles. The most disturbing Fall Out Boy video is probably "Saturday," since it features Pete as a crazed killer and Patrick as a pseudo-detective. The storyline includes a murder/suicide… always cheerful. But there are some exhilarating scenes of the band performing in a warehouse, redeeming the video from its gruesome storyline. The treatment for "Dead on Arrival" showcases the band in their van as they travel gig to gig, as well as some live performance shots. The video for "Grand Theft" shows the band having fun, playing their instruments out in the snow while a peeping tom looks through the window of a house to see his heart's desire dress for the day. In the end, he does get the girl – or more accurately, she gets him.

As the year wound down, *Alternative Press* named Fall Out Boy the second-most underrated band of the year, and they landed a spot on the magazine's list of "100 Bands You Need to Know" for 2004.

At this point, the pressure was building for the band, with nearly every reporter asking the members of Fall Out Boy to predict the future and guess where they'd be this time next year. Pete would have none of it, telling MTV, "My goal is just to keep going where it's at and never have any lofty expectations. I think a lot of bands get in trouble when they start having these expectations. For us, we never thought we would even play at this local club Fireside in our town, and then we played that and it just keeps on building. But this band is solely based on friendship, and as long as we keep being friends with each other, it'll keep getting better."

CHAPTER FIVE

THE NEVER-ENDING TOUR

In each band's life, they reach the point of no return. It's that volatile moment in time when the group's fortune could swing either way. With hard work, dedication and a monumental amount of touring, a band may get lucky enough to be noticed by the mainstream. Or not. But, without trying, no band would ever know if they had what it took to hang with the big boys. In 2004, Fall Out Boy knew what they had to do: tour incessantly and reach out to make sure *you* became a fan! They knew it wouldn't be easy, but it would be fun and if they made a few friends along the way, it would be well worth the effort.

This year the band wouldn't just play club dates. No, they moved on to multi-band showcases and package dates, like the Flipside Festival in Fairfax County, VA in April. Twenty-four bands played for nine hours straight on three different stages. Sugarcult headlined the event, with Fall Out Boy, Wakefield, Maxeen, Driving East, 33 West, Stars Hide Fire, Rude Buddha and Comma Effect providing backup.

To make sure the fans at home had something to remember them by while they were away on tour, on May 18 the band treated fans to an EP/DVD release titled *My Heart Will Always Be the B-Side to My Tongue*. Clever title! The all-acoustic EP was recorded at Chicago's Kingsize and Gravity studios during the early months of 2004 and was produced by the band and Sean O'Keefe, who also mixed the EP. The track list includes:

"My Heart is the Worst Kind of Weapon"
"It's Not a Side Effect of the Cocaine, I Am Thinking It Must Be Love"
"Nobody Puts Baby in the Corner"
"Love Will Tear Us Apart" (Joy Division cover)
"Grand Theft Autumn/Where Is Your Baby" (acoustic version)

A highlight of the release had to be Fall Out Boy's rendition of Joy Division's "Love Will Tear Us Apart." Classic. But true fans were more jazzed about the companion DVD that included a video bio/documentary, as well as videos, performance footage and other extras.

Fall Out Boy continued touring throughout the spring and summer of 2004 on their Believers Never Die tour and rolled into Austin's Stubb's club on July 14. Like so many other towns on their trek, the kids in town were thrilled that Fall Out Boy was playing locally and they turned out in record numbers. Before the show, Pete did an interview with *University Wire* and talked about the pressure to remain true to softcore pop-punk and to their fans: "At the end of the day, the only people who have ever liked our band are the kids," Pete said, "and they're the last people we are going to alienate, ever. It's sincerity with a hook. You come to the show, and you have the feel-good choruses and the kids having fun, but at the same time the people onstage are the same people offstage. There's a good chance you'll meet us and hang out, and hopefully you'll see that what we're doing is something we sincerely believe in. It's not a spectator sport when you catch a Fall Out Boy show."

"Who we are onstage is who we are offstage," Pete went on, "That could be said for some bands, and can't be said for every band. It's important to think about who you are supporting, what kind of music you support, what kind of artist you support and whether they're honest with you."

Pete was honored when *University Wire* told him that *Alternative Press* had called Fall Out Boy "saviors of pop-punk." But when asked about the band's upcoming studio album plans, he was a bit more introspective. "All of a sudden you go from recording in Joe's attic to having a bunch of 40-year-old guys with their jobs riding on what we're doing," Pete explained of their forthcoming venture with Island Records. "But we work best under pressure, and ultimately, we're competing against ourselves and not Thrice and Thursday.

"The first record was a product of tension," Pete went on to say. "We'd be at

each other's throat all the time and I was going to school like 40 hours a week. But we have already demoed like 12 songs and now we can focus completely on the music."

Of course, everyone and their sister wanted to know if Fall Out Boy planned to keep their toe-tapping rhythms and scathingly sarcastic lyrics. Pete told *University Wire*, "I think it would be stupid if we didn't stretch ourselves and try to do something a little different. We could put out *Take This to Your Grave 2* and play it safe, but at the same time you have to explore different things. It's not going to be loud and fast all the time."

But the new record would have to wait because Fall Out Boy had been selected to join this summer's Vans Warped Tour. While they were only playing a side stage to headliners like Taking Back Sunday and Coheed and Cambria, it was the perfect opportunity for the band to gain new fans and sharpen their onstage presence.

You'd think the band would want a break from touring after the summer's grueling Warped Tour, but no dice. These guys immediately headed out for a 29-date tour with headliners Taking Back Sunday. The journey began in Iowa City on September 28, 2004 at IMU. At the beginning of the tour, the band would bound out on stage to Joe Esposito's "You're the Best" from the movie *The Karate Kid*. Unfortunately, their audience of 10- to 20-year-olds was really too young to get the reference so they soon switched to playing Jay-Z tunes for their dramatic entrance.

Toward the end of December and into the New Year, you could find Fall Out Boy on the 42-city We Are Not Unique and Beautiful Snowflakes Tour with Gym Class Heroes and The Academy Is (some dates with Midtown and Silverstein as

well). One particular show stood out for FOB. It was at Manhattan's Irving Plaza on December 26, 2004. The band had just come off stage after their main set and were getting ready for their encore when their idol – and Island/Def Jam president – Jay-Z walked in. The band flipped and Jay-Z was pleased too, as he told *Spin*, "I went to see them at Irving Plaza and everyone knew the words and was singing. It was like a cult following. I watched them and thought, 'These guys are stars. This is genuine.'"

The band was riding high after that and finished out December with club gigs at the Electric Factory in

Philadelphia, House of Blues in Cleveland and both Metro and House of Blues in their hometown of Chicago.

It had been a big year for Fall Out Boy with two records on the airwaves and a list of past tour dates a mile long. Pete also had time to write and release a graphic novel with illustrator Joe Tesauro. Published by Pete's own company Clandestine Industries, the title – *The Boy with the Thorn in His Side* – tips its hat to The Smith's song of the same name. The story itself centered on a recurring nightmare Pete used to have as a child. (Pete wrote a second book, *Rainy Day Kids*, but it has yet to be published.)

While Fall Out Boy isn't the kind of band to take accolades too seriously, by the end of the year they were being thrown at them quite frequently. *Rolling Stone* named them one of the 10 Artists to Watch in 2005, as did MTV. They had finally cracked the code to success and had such a strong fan base it seemed logical that they'd explode in '05. The pressure to succeed was mounting though, and was about to take its toll on one of the members of the band.

CHAPTER SIX

HEAVY TIMES FOR PETE

January 2005 dawned and FOB found that their schedules weren't getting any lighter. All the guys felt stretched thin at this point. Suddenly, the great expectations for the year came to a screeching halt in February when it was announced that Pete had nearly overdosed on Ativan, a sedative used to treat anxiety. Had he tried to commit suicide? That's what everyone was saying, referencing the fact that he'd even previously told *Rolling Stone* that he'd had a fascination with the suicides of musicians Elliott Smith and Joy Division's Ian Curtis. Even Pete himself couldn't really refute the charge; he wasn't sure exactly what had happened. "It's so hard to think about and understand," he admitted later to *Rolling Stone*. "I'm not making an argument for being a disturbed genius; I was a confused kid."

Pete admitted to *Rolling Stone* that he began to feel the pressure and have panic attacks in 2004 during the recording of *From Under the Cork Tree*. "I started getting really crazy anxiety. I couldn't leave the house; I couldn't do anything. On the last record, you just wanted so bad for anyone to listen.

And with this record, all of a sudden it felt like everybody in the world was listening and was ready to pick apart every single word."

The overdose occurred right in Chicago in a Best Buy parking lot; Pete was sitting in his sister's Ford Escort at the time. Luckily, help arrived swiftly and, once his stomach was pumped, Pete was out of immediate danger. He was in the hospital for just about a week and decided to move home to his parents after his little escapade. Pete told told *Rolling Stone*, "My parents treat me like I'm 14. They make me clean my room and stuff like that. They're always like, 'I don't care what MTV says you are.'" That sort of grounding sentiment has helped Pete recover from his depression and anxiety.

While his band toured Europe with a substitute bass player, he entered therapy and even now when he's on the road, he'll call his therapist when he needs to regroup a bit. Talking with someone really helps as Pete told London's *Independent* newspaper, "I think – especially in America – that people don't realize it's okay to feel down and sad sometimes. It is part of the cycle of feeling okay. If you never feel sad, how do you know if you are okay?"

Even with the therapy and support of his family and friends, fans still know that Pete struggles with the same type of insecurities we all do. On his online journal, he wrote, "Sometimes it's hard to look in the mirror and feel okay with the person looking back." It's a sentiment each of us has probably grappled with at one time or another and, in some ways, it makes it a bit easier to know that someone like sexy rock star Pete Wentz feels like that too on occasion. His humility is part of the reason why we love this band so much and something Pete told the *Akron Beacon Journal* in 2006 confirms this, "There are the guys who walk around and are really sure they're the greatest thing in the world. And then there's us. We have all the same insecurities as the people that come to our shows."

Patrick admitted to the *San Jose Mercury News* that the band is just a bunch of misfits anyway, "We're basically four different clumps of nerds. We represent nerd sects. I'm not going to name names, but there's the spaz. There's the dweeb. There's the "Dungeons and Dragons" nerd. There's the guy who sits at the cool kids' table, but he totally goes home and knows all the words to some '80s chick flick." In the end, the only thing that matters is being true to yourself. As the band counsels at all their shows, be yourself and hang with your friends and you'll be okay.

CHAPTER SEVEN

FROM UNDER THE CORK TREE

With the support of his family, friends and bandmates, Pete started to live life again as normally as possible. Well, as normally as he could with *Take This to Your Grave* selling over 200,000 copies and a soon-to-be hit record about to be unleashed on the public! After all that touring last year, word of mouth had grown and just about everyone was anxiously awaiting Fall Out Boy's major-label debut album, *From Under the Cork Tree*. There was so much advance demand that Tower Records held a special pre-sale of the CD and ended up selling 2,500 copies in one day. That was a record for advance sales, besting presale figures from Thrice, Modest Mouse and Thursday. Tower was thrilled to tell anyone who would listen that Fall Out Boy's *From Under the Cork Tree* was its number one presale of all time.

That just fed the frenzy and fans lined up at their favorite record stores on May 3, 2005 to purchase a copy of *FUCT* (get it?), which took its name from a passage in Munro Leaf's children's book, *The Story of Ferdinand*. The story centers on Ferdinand the bull. Instead of being an aggressive, mean creature – as a child would perhaps expect of a large, scary-looking animal – Ferdinand was a pacifist. He preferred smelling the roses to getting in the ring and he spent his days thinking under the branches of a cork tree. Pete was incredibly moved by this, as he told Island Records during the making of *From Under the Cork Tree*. "I think it's an amazing metaphor for how people can be," he said. "There's something really honorable about following your own path and not doing what's expected of you." Bravo! "Ultimately," Pete explained to Nichole Farley of the *Kansas City Star*, "it [the album title] was just a symbol for pacifism at the time, and I think that it could mean so many different things. You're sitting right in the middle of one of the, I think, most misunderstood wars in recent history and I think that pacifism is a voice that needs to be heard." Pete was referring to the quagmire that U.S. president George W. Bush got America into when he went to war with Iraq in 2003 under dubious circumstances.

Even though this was the band's third full-length record, it was the first time they had the clout and backing of a major label behind them. *From Under the Cork Tree* – which would eventually see triple-Platinum sales – sold 68,000 copies in its first week and raced up the charts to debut at Number Nine on the *Billboard* 200.

After all the touring and stress of the last few years, the band could finally taste mainstream success! But Pete cautioned the *Fresno Bee* that fans should understand this wasn't overnight success, "People attribute a lot to overnight success. But a lot of people gloss over the fact that we were in a bus for three years. Our first record sold 300,000 without TV or radio."

From Under the Cork Tree had taken three months to record – from November 2004 through January 2005 – and it was all paying off now. "The last record we made in Madison, WI. We had to sleep on a girl's floor who we didn't even know – we had just met her when we got there," Pete acknowledged to MTV at the beginning of December 2004. "We ran out of cash halfway through the process. The studio would buy a six-pack of Sprite and a six-pack of Coke per week for us. So we asked them if they could buy us peanut butter and jelly instead. That's how we lived. The cool thing now is that we can just focus on the music. We don't have to worry about making money to live. We can all sleep in a bed at night."

Drummer Andy, for one, misses those old days. "Things were way more fun," he told MTV, "because it was more dangerous. You didn't know if you had a place to sleep. Now the only decision we have to make is which pool of money to sleep in." Not a terrible problem to have.

In interviews in 2004, all the band members stressed that they wanted their major-label debut to be different from *Take This to Your Grave*. "We wanted to write a record that was a lot more developed," Pete told MTV. "When we did *Take This to Your Grave*, we were really young, and it was like, make it or break it, this is your only shot. This time we had more time to sit with the songs and make them work and more of a chance to plan things out." That additional time proved to be very valuable since two weeks before the band went into the studio to record, they decided to scrap all the tunes they'd already written. They really wanted to try something new, so they sat down afresh and wrote a bunch of songs including the soon-to-be smash, "Sugar, We're Goin' Down."

Ultimately, the band just wanted to record an album that *they* liked. "We wrote a record that means a lot to us but maybe isn't going to mean a lot to the people who are hyping us as the next big thing," Pete cautioned MTV, "And that's fine. We don't want to be the saviors of anything – we just want to be ourselves." That's great advice for all of us, Pete!

Neal Avron produced *From Under the Cork Tree* at Burbank, CA's Ocean Studios. He'd worked with the Wallflowers, Everclear, Yellowcard and New Found Glory in the past and FOB was impressed with the sounds he was able to conjure from the recording console. Band and company moved over to Paramount Studios in Hollywood to mix the record, with the exception of several remixes that mix-master Tom Lord-Alge did at South Beach Studios in Miami. (Dan Dazinsky recorded "My Heart is the Worst Kind of Weapon" in Chicago back in 2003.) During the mastering phase, Brian "Big Bass" Gardner added his special touch at Bernie Grundman's facility in Los Angeles.

A departure for the band this time around was the fact that Pete wrote all the lyrics. Previously, Patrick would write the music and some lyrics and Pete would write the rest of the lyrics. The change came about as the result of an experiment. "It was an experiment that just worked out and I think that's how its gonna be from now on [Pete writing all lyrics]. It has a lot to do with inspiration and honesty," Patrick told Kent Bamberger of *HateSomethingBeautiful.com*, "and I have nothing to write about that's worth writing about. I'm totally happy. I've got no problems with anybody; my past year was great. Pete's last year was not so great. So he had a lot of stuff to write about and he's a better writer, so why not? I know a lot of people get weird about that because I'm the singer and I'm not writing the lyrics, but I'm writing the music so I'm definitely involved."

From the get-go, it looked like Fall Out Boy had a success on its hands.

According to the *Washington Post*, "*Cork Tree* is wordy and smart, successfully referencing everything from *Sixteen Candles* to *Casablanca*." [Actually, the *Casablanca* reference isn't what you think. It comes from *Windy City Heat*, an obscure film directed by comedian Bob Goldthwait.] The critics at *Rolling Stone*, that ever-so-tough-to-please music magazine, awarded the album 3 out of 5 stars.

So what was different about this record that made people sit up and take notice? "It's a little bit more introspective," Pete offered as speculation to MTV. "We're realizing where we are as a band and that no one's going to care three years from now what my girlfriend did to me." While the songs on *Take This to Your Grave* were inspired by infidelity, the new tunes touched upon broader themes.

The song list for *Cork Tree* shows FOB's penchant for lengthy titles that don't even reference the song lyrics! As Pete explained to Mark Guarino, music critic of the *Daily Herald*, "We were sick of seeing the typical one-word song titles [taken] from the chorus." Well, Fall Out Boy solved that problem. See for yourself:

"Our Lawyer Made Us Change the Name of This Song
So We Wouldn't Get Sued"

"Of All the Gin Joints in All the World"

"Dance, Dance"

"Sugar, We're Goin' Down"

"Nobody Puts Baby in the Corner"

"I've Got a Dark Alley and a Bad Idea That Says You Should Shut
Your Mouth (Summer Song)"

"7 Minutes in Heaven (Atavan Halen)"

"Sophomore Slump or Comeback of the Year"

"Champagne for My Real Friends, Real Pain for My Sham Friends"

"I Slept with Someone in Fall Out Boy and All I Got Was This
Stupid Song Written about Me"

"A Little Less Sixteen Candles, A Little More 'Touch Me'"

"Get Busy Living or Get Busy Dying (Do Your Part to Save
the Scene and Stop Going to Shows)"

"XO"

CHAPTER EIGHT

SINGLES AND VIDEOS

The first single released from the album was the infectious "Sugar, We're Goin' Down." Come on! Even your parents must hum along when this song comes on the radio! "Sugar" peaked at Number Eight on the *Billboard* Hot 100 and was honored several times by hitting Number One on MTV's *TRL*. With the popularity of the record, and the band growing, it's no wonder the album eventually went triple-Platinum!

"Sugar, We're Goin' Down" introduced Fall Out Boy to mainstream America. It was just about a perfect song, with the *Washington Post* referring to it as "…a not-quite-four-minute blast of cotton candy that's one of the summer's great singles."

Two versions of the single were released for sale: Part I was released with a green cover and B-side "The Music or the Misery." Part II, with B-sides "Dance, Dance (Patrick Stump Secret Agent Remix)", "Snitches and Talkers Get Stitches and Walkers" and "Sugar, We're Goin' Down (Concept Version)", was released with a red cover.

The video for "Sugar, We're Goin' Down" is just plain bizarre, and that's what Fall Out Boy loved about the idea when director Matt Lenski first proposed it. With the band's career taking off, they decided to put out a call for video ideas and dozens of directors threw their hats into the ring. Sadly, most of what FOB saw were rehashes of the same old pop-punk/emo video storyline. When they reviewed Lenski's submission, eyebrows were definitely raised. Pete explained to MTV, "It was the one treatment that really stood out. It was so strange. When I read it, it reminded me of Wes Anderson, like, 'Am I supposed to laugh at this, or is it depressing?'"

The video depicts the story of a boy – who has somehow grown deer antlers – who falls in love with a girl. The girl's father doesn't approve and chases said boy all over town, trying to kill him with a bow and arrow. During the chase, the father gets blindsided by a Jeep. When the boy doubles back to see what happened, he's astonished to find that the man has hooves! He's part deer too! The men bury the hatchet, as it were, and the father gives the couple his blessings. Oh yeah, and there are several bowling scenes thrown in for good measure. Huh? Like Fall Out Boy said, this is a weird story! Were the guys afraid to take the leap into such uncharted territory? Not necessarily. Pete told MTV, "A lot of emo bands, or pop-punk bands, they're afraid to be seen in a different light, or to be seen outside of some mold. But we're not like that at all. We don't take ourselves so seriously."

The Lenski treatment was actually the second video for "Sugar." The first one was hastily cobbled together by the record label and includes on-stage performance clips and some backstage footage. Once the "deer boy" video became available, it debuted on *TRL* and was embraced by MTV. In fact, on June 22 the video hit Number One on *TRL*, thanks to all the fans that voted for it!

Even though the video played constantly on MTV, the guys say they've never really seen the video the whole way through... and that's just the way they like it. "No matter where I'm watching TV, if I see the opening shot of our video, I will always turn it off, because I only think it breeds some insane kind of narcissism where you become obsessed with looking at yourself," Pete lectured to MTV in August of 2005. "It's kind of weird, it's kind of like when you hear your voice recorded on someone's answering machine and you're like, 'I sound like a moron!' But with the video it's worse. You're like, 'God, I *look* like such a moron!'"

The record's second single, and perhaps Fall Out Boy's most popular song to date, was "Dance, Dance." The song was released as a digital download, a CD and on 7-inch vinyl. "Dance, Dance" reached Number Eight on *Billboard*'s Pop 100 chart and eventually went double-Platinum. Some longtime fans immediately embraced the song while others were left scratching their heads and wondering if Fall Out Boy had sold out to commercialism. "The cool thing about 'Dance, Dance,'" Pete told MTV, "is that it's not afraid to have this rhythm that's dance-y. I think kids appreciate it, but people in emo and pop-punk bands are kind of scared by it. They're scared to have different rhythms that are a bit dancier and a bit '80s and a bit sexier. Not us. I think our motto could be, 'Don't be afraid to be sexy.'"

MTV called the video for "Dance, Dance" "an honest-to-goodness tribute to the spandex-and-synthesizer heyday of the 1980s." Patrick told the music channel, "We noticed a lot of bands referencing '80s music without really seeming to reference '80s music. And we love '80s music, so rather than just getting a synthesizer and jacking it, I just tried to write [David Bowie's] 'Modern Love.'"

The video for Dance, Dance" was filmed at Salesian High School in New Rochelle, NY (just outside of New York City). Alan Ferguson, who's also worked with Jay-Z and 112, directed the three-minute extravaganza that featured Fall Out Boy performing at a high school dance. Nerdy versions of themselves were also filmed attending said dance. Pete is featured in the video, of course, asking a girl for a date. "A Little Less Sixteen Candles a Little More 'Touch Me'" plays in the background while he chokes out his request.

Fall Out Boy really enjoyed making the videos and was glad there was an audience who was interested. "You're always making videos for MTV," Pete explained to Steve Knopper of *Rolling Stone*, "but you're no longer making them only for that – you're making them for Yahoo or AOL. MTV is where you're reaching your biggest audience. But it's always cool to reach an audience that's under the radar."

CHAPTER NINE

TOP OF
THE CHARTS

From *Under the Cork Tree* rocketed to the top of the charts within days of its release and on May 7, the band found themselves playing the home court and headlining at Chicago's Riviera Theatre. Despite the fact that U2, Nine Inch Nails and Coldplay were all also playing in Chicago that same weekend, Fall Out Boy still sold out the show in record time! There was no denying it now: Fall Out Boy had arrived. "It's all gone so much further than we ever thought it would," Pete told Jim DeRogatis of the *Chicago Sun-Times*. "I could've been working at Borders right now!" Fans across the world are so glad the guys didn't succumb to minimum-wage jobs!

Pete went on to talk with DeRogatis about how the music business has changed his life: "When I think about it, I went from 21 to 25, and the difference between me then and now is amazing. In the past two years, we've played over 500 shows. We've been to Manchester [England] and seen where Ian Curtis and The Smiths hung out. There are amazing sides of the music industry – people who have been dedicated for 30 or 40 years, people who believe in music – and there is the other side, people who are just snakes."

Still, Pete can't quite get used to being "famous." "All you wanted all your life is for someone to pay attention to you," he admitted to DeRogatis, "and all of a sudden the whole world is listening and it feels weird to be under the microscope. It's something you only thought about when you were 10, watching Axl Rose get off the bus in [the video for] 'Welcome to the Jungle,' and now you're living it."

On May 10, the band made their national TV debut on *Late Night with Conan O'Brien*. The next day the guys, in conjunction with Mastercard's Priceless Experience Internship program, announced the winners of a very special competition. Basically, Mastercard and Fall Out Boy were giving a dozen students the chance to help them prepare for and promote their live concert appearances during the upcoming Vans Warped Tour. These 12 lucky guys and gals spent a month prepping in Los Angeles before joining the Warped Tour and visiting Sacramento, CA; Boise, ID; Seattle, WA; and Portland, OR.

With the band's popularity growing, Fueled by Ramen decided to take advantage of the buzz and reissued a digitally remastered version of *Evening Out with Your Girlfriend* on May 17. Not only did they improve the sound quality, they also included a sampler CD with tracks from Project Rocket and The Kill Pill. This was perfect timing, as many new fans were boarding Fall Out Boy's train. Those same fans also came out in droves to watch MTV's *TRL* on May 24 when FOB's "Dance, Dance" video made its premier.

In June, a small snafu at MySpace gave the band a headache. It seemed that some people were impersonating them on the popular friendship/ networking site. As soon as FOB found out, they posted this notice on their website: "We have noticed a crazy amount of fake MySpace accounts for each of us. None of us have a personal MySpace account. We have also noticed a lot of people selling our autographs online. Don't support this. We promise that you can get our autographs at shows. Don't waste your money online."

Fall Out Boy had never been a fan of blogs and chatrooms, up to this point, and they even wrote a song called "I Liked You a Whole Lot Better Before You Became a Fucking MySpace Whore." Oh, come on guys, tell us how you really feel about MySpace?! So what exactly about these sites gets under FOB's collective skin? "It's about the idea that all of these online communities have become like collecting baseball cards," Pete told MTV in June of 2005. "My friend will say, 'Yeah, I got 89 million friends on the Internet,' And it's a bit of a meat market. A lot of people use the term

'MySpace hot,' like, 'Oh, she's hot in her picture, but she's only MySpace hot.'"

Fall Out Boy took care of the matter and MySpace shut down the offending imposter sites. Eventually, the band even launched their own MySpace page (see *MySpace.com/FallOutBoy*).

"The Internet has made it easier to interact with fans and easier to spread messages and get people out to shows," Pete went on to tell MTV. "But it works in reverse too, it's very easy to spread messages the other way." Unfortunately, the Internet would sting Pete again in the future when naked self-portraits he took to lure the attentions of a particular girl where snatched from his cell phone and transmitted across the Internet at light speed. Poor Pete! Imagine millions of people accessing photos of you nude!

In the middle of June, AOL Music started heavily promoting Fall Out Boy to 24.2 million music fans a month via its Breakers Program. Basically, AOL selects a band to feature and offered its listeners a CD listening party of *From Under the Cork Tree*, as well as other audio snippets and videos for the band's hit songs. It was a boon to the guys since it meant reaching different music fans, as Pete told *Business Wire*, "It's amazing that AOL chose us as part of the Breakers program. We feel that with their involvement, we can reach another level of fans who might not have heard us." Previous "Breakers" artists had included Josh Groban, The Game, Michelle Branch, John Legend and Sugarland.

The program did net the guys new fans and people were beginning to realize that this wasn't just amazing emo or softcore or pop-punk; this was amazing *music*!

CHAPTER TEN

HEADLINING VANS WARPED TOUR

The timing of the AOL promotion was perfect since on June 18, 2005, the band hit the road as one of the headliners of the summer's Vans Warped Tour. Kicking off at the Germain Amphitheater in Columbus, OH, FOB joined The Offspring, My Chemical Romance, Thrice, Transplants, Strung Out, MxPx, Dropkick Murphys, No Use for a Name, Atreyu, Mest, Hawthorne Heights and others as they crisscrossed the nation to play for hundreds of thousands of fans. "Warped Tour is cool," Patrick told *University Wire*, "because you get to see a lot of bands that you've either toured with before or have been dying to see. We get to see bands and we get to play – both those things are really fun. Every night there's a barbecue and you just hang out." Can we come join the party, Patrick? ; -)

Pete told the *Charlotte Observer* that, "Warped is very much about checking your ego at the door. Last year, we were traveling in a van, playing side stages. It could be frustrating at times, and we did get hazed a little bit. This year, we're upperclassmen. There's a little more respect for us now from the veterans of the tour." He went on to say that the event is truly about "camaraderie and

friendship. The only band we really compete with is My Chemical Romance, because we're both on the [*TRL*] countdown. But we're two completely different bands with two completely different points of view."

Does Pete have any pointers for fans who are new to attending a Warped show? Definitely. "Put on sunblock. When you get there, pick out the bands you want to see. Otherwise, you can kind of end up aimlessly walking around from stage to stage to stage, and by the middle of the day, you've already missed a lot. So many bands are playing at so many different times, you need a plan." That's solid advice.

As the Warped Tour rolled through the U.S., a third single from the album was released on July 5. "A Little Less Sixteen Candles, a Little More 'Touch Me'" may make your parents cringe, but the vampire-inspired video hit Number One on MTV's *TRL* on both May 5 and May 8, while the single reached Number 65 on *Billboard*'s Hot 100 and Number 38 on the U.K. singles chart. The single was released as a digital download, a CD and 7-inch vinyl disc.

Even as the Warped Tour was winding down in August, the band's PR machine was just warming up. This month, *Alternative Press* put the band on its cover and FOB found out that the single "Dance, Dance" would be included in Madden NFL 2006 videogame from Electronic Arts. And, to show just how popular the band was becoming, the search engine Lycos announced that "Fall Out Boy" was the 41st most popular search during the week of August 2, 2005.

Search activity for the band had actually increased 722 percent in the past month!

On August 15, the band played their last Warped show at Three County Fairgrounds in Northampton, MA. Despite the mud, terrible traffic and limited parking, fans toasted Fall Out Boy's success and the band ended the tour on a high note.

August 26 was the day fans could score a special limited edition gold vinyl version of *From Under the Cork Tree*. The run was limited to 500 copies and the only place to buy the collector's item was at *FueledbyRamen.com*. Packaged with the album were a couple of records by two bands that were signed to Pete's own record label, Decaydance. Fans were treated to music by Panic! At the Disco and the Hush Sound.

By August 28, the band was racing off to MTV's 22nd Annual Video Music Award in Miami. They were invited to play outside the American Airlines Arena during the "Pre-Show by the Shore." They treated the audience to a rendition of "Sugar, We're Goin' Down." Other special guests included Rihanna and hip-hop MCs Mike Jones, Paul Wall and Slim Thug. Despite the shadow of Hurricane Katrina – which hit Florida the Thursday before, killing several – the awards show was a success and Fall Out Boy went home having won the MTV2 Award for "Sugar, We're Goin' Down." Pete thought My Chemical Romance should have snagged the prize for their "Helena" video.

Of course, every time something really great happened for the band, something equally crappy had to be on the horizon. Anyone who follows music these days has probably heard the annoying patter of Brandon Flowers, lead singer of The Killers. Well, by the end of September 2005, he'd put Fall Out Boy in his sights and was badmouthing them at every turn. Quite annoying, actually, and Pete wouldn't stand for it.

Evidently, the riff started when Brandon mentioned in an interview that his band and FOB share the same A&R guy at Island, one Rob Stevenson. This struck Pete as a bit disingenuous and he wondered if The Killers were trying to compare themselves to FOB or put in a dig that since FOB had hit the big time, the staff at Island were a bit less receptive to the requests of their other less successful acts. Who knows? But, Pete wrote in his online journal, "It's funny the way you talk about sharing an A&R guy like it matters. It's too bad you wrote a couple of good songs, otherwise it'd be that much easier to write you off. I hope none of the other Las Vegas bands get jealous that there is another gem out in the middle of the desert." Well, that quote splattered across the Internet and the war of words between Brandon and Pete only intensified.

But, a lot of insiders said the beef was really blown out of proportion and that The Killers really had nothing against labelmates Fall Out Boy. Ronnie Vannucci, drummer for The Killers, told MTV, "Everybody's got an opinion and if someone asks [Brandon] something, he's going to say it. We don't always agree with him, but that's his prerogative. I think this falls along the same lines. I hadn't even heard about this thing with Fall Out Boy until a few days ago, and I still don't get it. We got nothing against those guys at all. And, I kind of like that song they've got ['Sugar, We're Goin' Down']. It's catchy."

The matter was soon put to rest and the bands called a truce, but not before Pete and Patrick wrote a song, "You Can't Spell 'Star' without A&R," about the situation.

Fall Out Boy then had about a month off before they embarked on a 40-date U.S. jaunt as part of the 2005 Nintendo Fusion Tour. They kicked off in Detroit with The Starting Line, Motion City Soundtrack, Boys Night Out and Panic! At the Disco. "It's our first big headlining tour," Pete told MTV, "and you can't really find a better sponsor as far as Nintendo is concerned. They pretty much just stay out of the way and let us do whatever we want." The package tour itself is popular since one low-ticket price assures you access to see a bunch of great bands and a chance to check out new, cool video games from Nintendo. Since the band members are self-proclaimed video game nerds, this tour would prove to be very enjoyable for them.

During the tour, the band found out that *From Under the Cork Tree* was certified Gold! It was terrific news and they celebrated at a sold-out show at Chicago's Aragon Ballroom. It was a fantastic way to enjoy their success with the fans that have been behind them since the beginning.

By October, demand for Fall Out Boy tickets was growing and the quartet had to book larger venues as a result. On October 8, they were playing Tsongas Arena in the old mill town of Lowell, MA. "We wouldn't play an arena just to say we played an arena," Pete assured his fans. "There was a really high demand for tickets in Boston, so we decided to play a room that could fit as many of our fans as possible."

In the middle of the month, MTV's *TRL* premiered the band's '80s-centric video for "Dance, Dance." The single and video were being played constantly on radio, TV and online, but FOB wasn't about to rest on their laurels. They wanted to start work on the next record. "If you look at guys in hip-hop and R&B, they just put out record after record, and they just churn out intelligent music," Pete told MTV. "That's part of what's been wrong with the rock industry; they keep fans waiting far too long and bands go away and disappear off the face of the planet. That's not the way it's going to be for Fall Out Boy."

In fact, Fall Out Boy had already put considerable thought into who they'd like to get as producer for their next record. Pete told MTV, "The guy we really want and we're trying to lock it down with is very bizarre for Fall Out Boy. It's Babyface. He said he wants to do it, but nothing's confined yet." Babyface is known for producing smooth and successful R&B, but FOB heard something in his work that they felt could cross over and be beneficial to their next record.

While the band wouldn't be able to go into the studio for awhile to record another full-length album, in November they were given the opportunity to record "raw" versions of several songs – "Sugar, We're Goin' Down," "Dance, Dance," "Our Lawyer Made Us Change the Name of This Song So We Won't Get Sued" and "Grand Theft Autum/Where Is Your Boy?" – for Clear Channel Radio's *Stripped Raw and Real* series. They also recorded a version of Joy Division's "Love Will Tear Us Apart." The tracks were available on 130 Clear Channel radio station websites, as well as *StrippedMusic.com*.

The end-of-year accolades started pouring in for Fall Out Boy on November 9 at the 2005 mtvU Woodie Awards, held at Roseland Ballroom in New York City. College students voiced their preferences and awarded FOB the Road Woodie for Best Tour of the Year. The band also got involved with the production of the awards themselves when they assisted David Melillo, an artist and student at Valencia Community College in Florida, with composing the ceremony's original score. Fall Out Boy attended the ceremony and then went back out on the road to close the Nintendo Fusion tour on the 23rd. Another pat on the back for the guys arrived on December 5 when they won the Emerging Artist Award from XM Satellite Radio's XM Nation Music Awards. Almost one-and-a-half million subscribers voted!

Then, like so many other hardcore/pop-punk acts before them, they played KROQ's Acoustic Christmas show in Los Angeles as the holidays approached. Nine Inch Nails headlined. On December 14, the boys found themselves in Virginia to play radio station FM 106.1 The Zone's winter concert. Then the band geared up for a quiet New Year's Eve… by playing in Times Square as guests on MTV's New Year's Eve show, along with Kanye West, Shakira and Nelly!

The world was definitely spinning a bit faster for Fall Out Boy. Yet, for every two steps forward, they seemed to take one step back. *From Under the Cork Tree* sold over one million records this year. Yet, *Spin*'s year-end poll dubbed them Worst Band of the Year. What?! Pete shrugged that off and told the *Kansas City Star*, "I think backlash is somewhat expected, because everybody wants a band that they can keep in their back pocket and can be their secret, and as a band grows it's like growing pains. It's impossible not to have them"

The hardcore audience may have been split, but it was clear that the majority of America loved what Fall Out Boy was doing. Now it was time to conquer the rest of the world.

CHAPTER ELEVEN

NEW YEAR, MORE TOURING

Fall Out Boy rang in 2006 with some shows in the U.K. before returning to the States to begin their Black Clouds and Underdogs Tour in support of *From Under the Cork Tree*, which by this point had sold 1.6 million copies. On some 50-odd dates, All-American Rejects, Hawthorne Heights and From First to Last opened for Fall Out Boy. Besides the scheduled dates, the band offered the chance for fans to win a free show in their own town. All they had to do was join *MyLocalBands.com*, a Friendster-type site, and recruit other friends and fans to join. The city with the most activity would win a free show. The tour started on March 15 in Albany, NY. Fall Out Boy was adamant about keeping ticket prices down on this tour and every ticket, no matter in which city, was under $30. "We've gradually played in front of 50,000 to 80,000 people due to demand," Pete told the *Chicago Sun*. "We wanted to play arenas at this point to give everybody a chance to see us, but our next U.S. tour after this will probably be a small club tour."

For Patrick it was super-important to keep the shows affordable. "I remember being a kid wanting to go to shows but not being able to afford it," he told the

FALL OUT BOY AND ITS FIRST GRAMMY NOM!

In 2006, the band was nominated for its first Grammy in the Best New Artist category. They were up against Ciara, Keane, Sugarland and John Legend. All tough competition. They lost out to Legend who received his award at the 48th Annual Grammy Awards ceremony on February 8 at the Los Angeles Staples Center. Boo! But what do you expect from an award's show that's decided by industry old-timers and not the fans themselves? It will make you feel better to know, however, that in the annual Harris Interactive YouthQuery Survey that let teens vote for their favorite artist, Fall Out Boy won with 30 percent of the vote. Ciara snagged 21 percent, Sugarland got eight percent, John Legend with six percent and Keane went home with just five percent. The band didn't seem too disappointed that they didn't win. Patrick said the best thing about getting nominated for a Grammy was the respect they received from their parents. "They are finally okay with us not going to college," Patrick told *Rolling Stone*. The band and their families attended the awards ceremony together.

Portland Press. "Like [bands] don't make enough money. It's just stupid. It's an uphill battle, but we like to do what we can to keep [ticket prices] low."

To rev up excitement before the Grammy's, in which Fall Out Boy had been nominated for Best New Artist, the band made a number of promotional appearances. They were on the cover of *Spin* magazine and visited with David Letterman on January 2. From there, the band jetted off for a few European dates before returning to play an all ages show at the House of Blues in Los Angeles on February 6, just two days before the Grammy winners would be announced. Fall Out Boy was ultimately shut out at the Grammy's – John Legend won Best New Artist – but the guys felt honored just to be nominated.

On February 25, the band appeared along with Mariah Carey, Bono, Madonna, Kanye West, Christina Aguilera, My Chemical Romance and others at

MTV's 4th Annual TRL Awards. FOB was nominated for and won Best New Artist against Ciara, Chris Brown and My Chemical Romance. They were also nominated for Best Group That Actually Plays Instruments, against The Killers, My Chem, Green Day and Simple Plan. My Chem went home with that trophy.

March came in like a lion and fate would deal Pete a pretty embarrassing blow when photos of his penis surfaced on the Internet after the files were stolen from his T-Mobile Sidekick. What made the situation worse was the fact that he took the photos himself! Why in the world would someone do that? Well, he was trying to impress a girl and thought his, umm, girth would do the trick. The plan backfired when the photos were jacked and posted to the Internet by that very woman for millions of people to see. Let's be honest, you took a peek didn't you?

"I was initially shocked," Pete told the *Fresno Bee* when he realized the girl of his dreams betrayed him and posted pictures of his privates to the 'Net. "Then it

was kinda like, 'Why would anybody care about any goofy dude from the suburbs of Chicago?' From there I just laughed about it. At the same time, if you don't want pictures of yourself on the Internet, you shouldn't take pictures like that."

He does regret that happened, as he told the *Minneapolis Star Tribune*, "To be honest, I'd rather not have three million people see me naked. People would say, 'Any press is good press.' In retrospect, it's easy to say that. But I freaked out when it happened. It was really bad. If I could rewind it and not have it happen, it would definitely be the decision I would make. But, at the same time, there's a lot of things you do that you have to live with."

The timing was awful because the band was playing a super intimate show at New York's Knitting Factory on March 3. This was one of their "secret shows,"

meant to thank area fans. They were billed as Saved Latin, but everyone knew it was really a Fall Out Boy show. Skyriter and Valencia opened the show and lots of other famous musicians attended the fete, including My Chemical Romance's bassist Mikey Way, who even joined the band onstage during "Dance, Dance." Midtown singer Gabe Saporta was there, along with drummer Rob Hitt. Gym Class Heroes' Travis McCoy introduced the band. Things didn't look up for Pete when he did a stage dive and no one caught him. Damn! He recovered what he could of his dignity and they closed with the perennial "Saturday." The following evening, the band appeared on *Saturday Night Live*.

On March 13, the press-shy Patrick appeared on MTV's *TRL* at their Times Square Studios for the world premiere of the video for "A Little Less 16 Candles, A Little More 'Touch Me.'" Was Pete still recovering from the world seeing him naked? MTV Overdrive, the broadband network, simultaneously premiered the video and made it available exclusively on-demand for 24 hours following the premiere.

The next day, the limited Black Clouds and Underdogs edition of *From*

Under the Cork Tree was released. It featured five additional tracks, remixes of "Sugar, We're Goin' Down" and "Dance, Dance" (the exclusive iTunes version also includes their video retrospective). The extras included:

"Snitches and Talkers Get Stitches and Walkers"
"The Music or the Misery"
"My Heart is the Worst Kind of Weapon" (demo)
"Sugar, We're Goin' Down" (Patrick Stump remix)
"Dance, Dance" (Lindbergh Palace remix)

Continuing on the theme, the band's next tour – starting on March 15 at the Pepsi Arena in Albany, NY – was dubbed the Black Clouds and Underdogs Tour. They appeared with All-American Rejects, Hawthorne Heights and From First to Last. For this tour, FOB added some pyrotechnics to the mix during "Sugar, We're Goin' Down." The band was especially lively on stage during this tour and usually closed with the crowd pleaser, "Saturday." It was tough to score a ticket though because most shows on this arena tour sold out! Fall Out Boy played their hearts out to about 8,000 fans every night.

Music lovers that couldn't snare a seat at a show were able to view a special on MTV called *Fall Out Boy On Tour*. The program showed concert footage, along with scenes of backstage mayhem. No substitute for a concert, but it was better than nothing for some desperate fans.

The rest of the spring was a whirlwind on the road with standout shows at

The Joint in Las Vegas on March 30 and an appearance on *The Tonight Show with Jay Leno* on April 3. Fall Out Boy even hit Bamboozle 2006 at the Meadowlands in East Rutherford, NJ at the beginning of May. One hundred bands played over two days on five stages.

FOB played part in a bit of a controversy in May when a fan's mom attended a show in Charlotte, NC and was disgusted by their behavior. What offended her so much? The band's "homosexual rally." Umm, was she listening to what the guys said at all or was she just on crank? The entire band, and Pete especially, is always talking about individuality and accepting people and not being homophobic. The mom's letter was posted to Fall Out Boy's website and read, in part, "The ticket said 'all ages'…and your band was very foul mouthed and anti-morals. I didn't spend over $200 for tickets, gas, food and unforturnately [sic] shirts that I purchased for them before the concert, for you to give your own personal political testimony, cursing anyone who disagreed. This was a concert, not some liberal homosexual rally."

Pete responded on the band's website, writing, "the only thing I said in Charlotte was (quoted word for word): 'you can leave this show and say I think this guy is an arrogant jerk. Or think this band is better than this one – because these are your opinions – I understand that. The only thing we consider unacceptable is for you to engage in sexist, racist or homophobic behavior. If you do and want to continue to, we don't want you as a fan."

He went on to say, "I encourage fans of our band to grow up to become good people and to change the world. Unfortunately, I don't believe that treating other people as inhuman is acceptable."

Despite the hateful diatribe from the anonymous woman, the band continued to tour to thousands of happy fans, closing up shop on May 13 at Toronto's

Ricoh Coliseum. From there, the band caught a plane to Europe for a U.K. tour that included a stop at Manchester's Apollo, the Brixton Academy, a headline gig at the Leeds Slam Dunk Festival at Millennium Square, the Corn Exchange in Edinburgh and the Wolverhampton Civic Hall in the U.K.

On June 2, the band played a spectacular homecoming show in Chicago at the Logan Square Auditorium. The show as a spur-of-the-moment decision and tickets were given away free as a thank-you to everyone who's supported them locally over the years. It was a success and a very special way to end the tour.

Over the next few weeks, the band took some time off and prepared to go into the studio for their next album. Despite all the press about Pete being a momma's boy, he actually bought a house in Los Angeles, and an English bulldog named Hemingway to go with it! Whether he'll be a full-time California resident remains to be seen.

August held two key events for the band: the Teen Choice Awards and MTV's Video Music Awards. Fall Out Boy won a triple-header at the 2006 Teen Choice Awards: Best Single for "Dance, Dance," Best Rock Group and Best Rock Track (also for "Dance, Dance").

On the 31st, the band appeared at Radio City Music Hall in New York City as presenters at the 2006 MTV Video Music Awards. They sported Victorian-inspired outfits with scarves and hankies. Pete even wore a cloak designed by Dolce & Gabbana. Stranger than their attire was the fact that the band brought a monkey with them as they walked down the red carpet and into the show! Some of the highlight performers included Panic! At the Disco, The Killers and The All-American Rejects. Jack Black hosted the show. Our boys were nominated in two categories: Best Group Video for "Dance, Dance" and Viewer's Choice.

In the video category, they were up against some stiff competition with All-American Rejects' "Move Along," Gnarls Barkley's "Crazy," Panic! At the Disco's "I Write Sins Not Tragedies" and Red Hot Chili Peppers "Dani California." Fall Out Boy didn't win, but they were psyched anyway because their friends Panic! *did* win! It was especially meaningful for Pete since he signed the band to his own Decaydance record label. FOB did snag the Viewer's Choice award for "Dance, Dance" away from Chris Brown with Juelz Santana, Kelly Clarkson, Rihanna and Shakira with Wyclef Jean.

By the fall, rumors about a new FOB record were swirling fast and furiously. "We're probably about halfway through [making the record] and it's awesome," Patrick told MTV in September. "When we were writing this record, I felt like there's no point in trying to pretend like we're a band we're not. We're just gonna go in and make our record the way we're gonna make it."

Producer Neal Avron, who worked with the band on *From Under the Cork Tree*, is at the helm again. And, as FOB had hoped, Babyface would provide some production assistance. Pete had to take some time away from the record so he could attend Fashion Week in New York and showcase his new line of clothing from Clandestine Industries: think cool hoodies and short shorts. Lots of industry all-stars attended his showcase, including Paris Hilton, Russell Simmons, Ryan Cabrera and Lauren "LC" Conrad of *The Hills* and *Laguna Beach*.

Pete was eager to get back to L.A. to finish recording though, as he told MTV, "All the guitar, drum and bass parts have been laid down, and now we're working on vocals. We've done all 14 songs we were supposed to do with Neal, and then in October we're going to do two songs with Babyface." That they did, and Pete and company really enjoyed the experience, telling MTV, "Working with Babyface has been cool, different. The hours are way better. We work from, like, 3 pm till midnight. One night we even started at midnight. Kind of amazing for us late sleepers."

News soon leaked from Island Records that the album, *Infinity on High*, was slated for a February 6, 2007 release date. However, one song, "The Carpal Tunnel of Love" was streamed at *AbsolutePunk.net* on November 9. This isn't the first official single to herald the record, but rather a first taste of the new music courtesy of FOB. Fans were ecstatic and were thankful that the band made that decision. (The band, and not their record label, provided the song for streaming and Island, in fact, wasn't even aware of the plan.)

Even more exciting, Chicago radio station Q101 was first to play "This Ain't a Scene, It's an Arms Race" on November 16. The fist-pumping single was soon thereafter leaked to the Internet. The tune is about Pete's continued frustration with the growing emo scene. He told *Rolling Stone*, "There may be other songs on the record that would be bigger radio hits, but this one had the right message." The next day, the song was available on *FriendsorEnemies.com*. Finally, on November 21, the single was officially released and marked the countdown to the new album.

The 2006 American Music Awards on November 21 turned out to be the perfect venue for the band to debut the live version of "This Ain't a Scene, It's an Arms Race" and the song shipped to radio that night. You can bet it was spinning like crazy on stations all over the U.S. for the rest of the month!

After all this excitement, the band shuttled back to L.A. to shoot the video for "This Ain't a Scene, It's an Arms Race" between November 29 and December 1. By the 19th it was ready for its premier. These guys work fast! The video will definitely make you smile. We see the band recording in the studio with some hip-hop producers. As Patrick sings his heart out, the producer and posse give each other looks, shake their heads and start to laugh. The guys in Fall Out Boy are getting a bit nervous but they put their all into it and, eventually, the posse gets into the music. That is, until Joe twirls with his guitar and busts the beers for the evening! The band get beat up and tossed out. Throughout the video, scenes of a wild party in a hotel room cut in and out. A photo shoot with Pete as the model is also a focus of the video and – oops! – he gets overexposed *again*! Viewers are then back in the hotel room where the band is clowning around, jumping on a bed until, horror of all horrors, Pete falls out the window to his death. We then segue to Patrick and band singing and playing at Pete's funeral.

As the video comes to a close, the casket opens and Pete sits up. It's then clear that this has all been a dream and the band is back in Des Moines, IA in 2003 getting ready for a gig.

In mid-December, Fall Out Boy once again visited AOL Music and played three new songs, including the first single from *Infinity on High*, "This Ain't a Scene, It's an Arms Race," in addition to "Thriller" and "The Takeover, The Break's Over." They closed with their hit, "Sugar, We're Goin' Down."

Around the same time, the band found out they won The Napster Award for "Most-Played Song of the Year" with "Dance, Dance." Big surprise! It's no wonder then that Fall Out Boy would be partying to end the year with a bang. It's no wonder that the guys in Fall Out Boy found themselves once again performing at MTV's Times Square bash in Manhattan, partying and ending the year with a bang.

Once again, Fall Out Boy found itself at a pivotal point in its career. Would their second major-label album be a success or a sophomore slump? The pressure was pushing down on all the band members but they weren't worried. They truly believed in the songs they recorded for *Infinity on High* and they were looking forward to getting back out on the road to introduce their fans to the new music. As long as the band was content with the record and their core fans understood how hard they had worked on this follow-up, FOB figured everything would be okay. 2007, here we come!

CHAPTER TWELVE

FRIENDS
OR ENEMIES

It would be weird if Fall Out Boy didn't begin the year with a tour. After all, these guys have basically spent the last five years of their lives out on the road! And so, its no surprise FOB hit the streets for their Friends or Enemies club tour. Yes, the band was finally getting back to its roots and playing some smaller venues, as they'd been hoping to for the past year. This was the first opportunity that allowed them the freedom to do it. New Found Glory joined them on the road, as did Early November, Permanent Me and Lifetime.

Halfway through the tour, the band couldn't resist heading home to Chicago on January 21 to play the halftime show at the NFC Championship game at Soldier Field. They had to support the Bears as they went up against the New Orleans Saints!

The U.S. leg was a short one and hit less than two-dozen major cities during the month of January, starting in San Francisco and closing in Orlando. Fall Out Boy focused their set on tunes off *From Under the Cork Tree* but did tease fans with a new track or two from their forthcoming album, *Infinity on High* (due in stores February 6). In fact, they closed their set with the first single from that

GET THE 911 ON FOB

FallOutBoyRock.com
The official website packed with tour dates, photos,
Pete's journal and more.

MySpace.com/FallOutBoy
Their official presence at this networking haven.

FriendsorEnemies.com
Don't miss Joe Trohman's journal
where he includes a "Sick Riff of the
Week" for you aspiring guitarists.

OvercastKids.com
Home base for the official Fall Out Boy fan club.

FueledbyRamen.com
The band's first record label.

IslandRecords.com
The band's current record label. Search for "Fall Out Boy."

ClandestineIndustries.com
Pete's company that sells clothing, books and more.

Decaydance.com
Pete's record label (an imprint of Fueled by
Ramen). (Pete signed Panic! At the Disco and issued
legend Lifetime's "comeback" songs after a
10-year absence on the scene.

album, "This Ain't a Scene, It's an Arms Race."

Speaking of "This Ain't a Scene," the video for the single hit Number One on MTV's *TRL* on January 8!

After the U.S. leg of the tour, the band headed off to Europe to play to fans in the U.K., Germany, France, Sweden, Denmark and the Netherlands. In between dates, they even found a way to make the trip to Japan for a concert in Osaka and one in Tokyo. (These guys must have a zillion frequent flier miles!)

In March, Australian fans were treated to the first ever Fall Out Boy tour in their country. The band made the most of just three dates Down Under at the Vodafone Arena in Melbourne on March 7, the Hordern Pavilion in Sydney on the 8th and the Convention Centre in Brisbane on the 10th.

CHAPTER THIRTEEN

INFINITY ON HIGH

On February 6, 2007 in the U.S. (a day earlier in the U.K.), Fall Out Boy fans will rush home from the record store clutching the band's latest album, *Infinity on High*. As they cue up the CD, they'll wonder just what they're in store for. Then it will happen. Jay-Z's voice will thunder from their speakers, cascading over a bed of electric guitars. He'll chastise the critics who said he had no business collaborating with Fall Out Boy and thank the fans for supporting the band. After all, not only is Jay-Z one of today's top recording artists himself, he's also the president of Island/Def Jam, the record label home of FOB. But does he belong on their record?

The band thought so and was jazzed that Jay-Z agreed to take part in the album; they had been wishing that he would for the past year! Pete told MTV, "It's so important to begin strong, and I don't think you can start much stronger than this. This is a message recorded directly to our fans – it's one of the few times on the record where we speak directly to them, and I think it's amazing that Jay is having a conversation with our fans. Also, it's a snapshot of where we are right now. And years from now, when I'm laying in some gutter somewhere, Jay-Z will still be on this record." Pete, we really hope you're kidding about the gutter part!

By the time the record is released, fans will have already heard a lot about it through the grapevine that is the Internet. Pete's been telling just about everyone that the album title is a reference to Vincent van Gogh. The phrase *infinity on high* was actually taken from a letter the painter wrote to his brother Theo in 1888: "Be clearly aware of the stars and infinity on high. Then life seems almost enchanted after all."

Neal Avron – who worked on *From Under the Cork Tree* – produced most of *Infinity on High*, with Babyface also tackling several tracks. Still, everyone wondered if the follow-up to *Cork Tree* would elicit the same kind of enthusiasm. After all, their last album sold three million copies!

The first single that was released in November 2006, "This Ain't a Scene, It's an Arms Race," is about the punk scene. As Pete told MTV, "It's just kind of a tongue-in-cheek look at the way we are so addicted and obsessed with new arts, cultures and loves – to the point where it just becomes oversaturated. I think people are gonna read into it what they will. In the back of my head, it's a call to arms – more in the way that you sometimes need to just talk to yourself in the mirror." It's hard to keep still when you hear this song; you just want to jump up and dance whenever you hear it.

It's too early to know the full impact this album will have on Fall Out Boy's career and the pop-punk scene in general. However, if early praise is any indication, the band will enjoy another terrific year. It's early 2007 and FOB fans have a major tour to look forward to.

While the band's Friends or Enemies tour closes in Scotland on April 4, by the 18th they'll be ready to kick off a major 2007 U.S. tour in Charlotte, NC. Their sponsor this time out will be Honda and they'll headline the car manufacturer's 7th Annual Honda Civic Tour. The band, together with Honda, designed a special edition Honda Civic Hybrid that's being showcased at each concert during the tour. One lucky fan will win the vehicle by tour's end! The ride features cool Fall Out Boy graphics, hemp upholstery and an Alpine sound system that's loaded with personal messages from Pete.

So all you fans out there need to buy *Infinity on High* right now, snag tickets to Fall Out Boy's next show in your town and get ready to crowd surf!

chapter fourteen

THE FOB STATE
OF THE UNION

Fall Out Boy has never had a master plan and it's never been about world domination of the music scene. But maybe that's been the key to their success. These four unassuming guys from Chicago have no false pretenses about them. They are who they are and they're music is honest, invigorating and *fun*. And *that's* what it's all about!

Of course the band has had their struggles and disappointments – who hasn't – but they believe in themselves and their fans. That's why they formed a punk band in the first place as Pete told the *Minneapolis Star Tribune*, "Your initial goal is to never have a real job so you can always spend time with your friends and your family and never have any real responsibility. That's why you do a band. [But] you end up with more responsibility and a bigger job than you've ever planned on. You've put yourself in a spot where everyone is going to watch you make missteps and everyone is going to watch you complain about it. My life is good and really easy compared to people in Iraq who get bombed every single day. The thing I have to worry about is whether I have diet or regular soda in our [dressing room]."

While he may be simplifying things a bit, his message is clear. Go after your dream and you'll be successful just for trying. Life is good if you just accept it.

The band, and Pete in particular, are philosophic on the state of their celebrity today. As he told MTV back in 2005, "Fall Out Boy has never been about goals or ambitions. We started out just for fun, and it became this huge thing. I'd love to keep everything going, but if it all ended today, at least it went all these places it was never supposed to go in the first place."

The journey has been what matters most to

Pete, Patrick, Joe and Andy, and with any luck, these four cool kids from Chicago will keep singing and inspiring fans for years to come.

DISCOGRAPHY

EPs

Project Rocket / Fall Out Boy Split EP
May 28, 2002 (Uprising Records)
"Growing Up"
"Switchblades and Infidelity"
"Moving Pictures"
Note: This EP also included three songs from Project Rocket.

My Heart Will Always Be the B-Side to My Tongue
May 18, 2004 (Fueled by Ramen)
"My Heart Is The Worst Kind Of Weapon" (acoustic)
"It's Not A Side Effect Of The Cocaine, I Am Thinking It Must Be Love"
"Nobody Puts Baby In The Corner"
"Love Will Tear Us Apart"
"Grand Theft Autumn / Where Is Your Boy" (acoustic)

ALBUMS

An Evening Out With Your Girlfriend
March 25, 2003 (Uprising Records)
"Honorable Mention"
"Calm Before The Storm"
"Switchblades and Infidelity"

"Pretty In Punk"
"Growing Up"
"The World's Not Waiting (For Five Tired Boys IN a Broken Down Van)"
"Short, Fast and Loud"
"Moving Pictures"
"Parker Lewis Can't Lose (But I'm Gonna Give It My Best Shot)"

Take This to Your Grave
May 6, 2003 (Fueled by Ramen)
"Tell That Mick He Just Made My List Of Things To Do Today"
"Dead On Arrival"
"Grand Theft Autumn/Where Is Your Boy"
"Saturday"
"Homesick At Space Camp"
"Sending Postcards From A Plane Crash (Wish You Were Here)"
"Chicago Is So Two Years Ago"
"The Pros And Cons Of Breathing"
"Grenade Jumper"
"Calm Before The Storm"
"Reinventing The Wheel To Run Myself Over"
"The Patron Saint Of Liars And Fakes"

From Under the Cork Tree
May 3, 2005 (Island Records)
"Our Lawyer Made Us Change The Name Of This Song So We Wouldn't Get Sued"
"Of All The Gin Joints In All The World"

"Dance, Dance"

"Sugar, We're Goin' Down"

"Nobody Puts Baby In The Corner"

"I've Got A Dark Alley And A Bad Idea That Says You Should Shut Your Mouth (Summer Song)"

"7 Minutes In Heaven (Atavan Halen)"

"Sophomore Slump Or Comeback Of The Year"

"Champagne For My Real Friends, Real Pain For My Sham Friends"

"I Slept With Someone In Fall Out Boy And All I Got Was This Stupid Song Written About Me"

"A Little Less Sixteen Candles, A Little More 'Touch Me'"

"Get Busy Living or Get Busy Dying (Do Your Part To Save The Scene And Stop Going To Shows)"

"XO"

From Under the Cork Tree – Limited Black Clouds and Underdogs Edition
March 14, 2006 (Island Records)

"Our Lawyer Made Us Change the Name of This Song So We Wouldn't Get Sued"

"Of All the Gin Joints in All the World"

"Dance, Dance"

"Sugar, We're Goin' Down"

"Nobody Puts Baby in the Corner"

"I've Got a Dark Alley and a Bad Idea That Says You Should Shut Your Mouth (Summer Song)"

"7 Minutes in Heaven (Atavan Halen)"

"Sophomore Slump or Comeback of the Year"

"Champagne for My Real Friends, Real Pain for My Sham Friends"

"I Slept with Someone in Fall out Boy and All I Got Was This Stupid Song Written About Me"

"Little Less Sixteen Candles, A Little More 'Touch Me'"

"Get Busy Living or Get Busy Dying (Do Your Part to Save the Scene and Stop Going To Shows)"

"XO"

"Snitches and Talkers Get Stitches and Walkers"

"Music or the Misery"

"My Heart Is the Worst Kind of Weapon" (demo version)

"Sugar, We're Goin' Down" (Patrick Stump Remix)

"Dance, Dance" (Lindbergh Palace Remix)

Infinity on High
February 6, 2007 (Island Records)

"Thriller"

"The Take Over, The Breaks Over"

"This Ain't a Scene, It's an Arms Race"

"I'm Like a Lawyer with the Way I'm Always Trying to Get You Off (Me & You)"

"Hum Hallelujah"

"Golden"

"Thnks fr th Mmrs"

"Don't You Know Who I Think I Am?"

"The (After) Life of the Party"

"The Carpal Tunnel of Love"

"Bang the Doldrums"

"Fame < Infamy"

"You're Crashing, But You've No Wave"

"I've Got All This Ringing In My Ears and None On My Fingers"